WE ARE THE EARTH

Bobbie Kalman

🌳 **Crabtree Publishing Company**

www.crabtreebooks.com

Created by
Bobbie Kalman

Inspired by Dr. David Suzuki,
for whom I have the greatest admiration!

Author and Editor-in-Chief
Bobbie Kalman

Editor
Kathy Middleton

Proofreader
Crystal Sikkens

Photo research
Bobbie Kalman

Design
Bobbie Kalman
Katherine Berti
Samantha Crabtree (cover)

Production coordinator
Katherine Berti

Illustrations
Barbara Bedell: pages 1 (leaves and flower), 15 (tuatara), 19,
    20 (mushrooms), 28
Katherine Berti: page 21 (termites)
Jeannette McNaughton-Julich: page 21 (termite mound)
Bonna Rouse: page 20 (hyphae)
Margaret Amy Salter: page 1 (butterflies)

Photographs
© Dreamstime.com: page 22 (bottom except world)
© iStockphoto.com: front cover (children), pages 23, 26 (top and bottom
    left), 27 (top left), 28 (top), 29 (top left and bottom right children), 30
© Photos.com: page 21 (right)
© Shutterstock.com: front and back covers (except children), pages 1, 3,
    4, 5, 6, 7, 8, 9 (bottom), 10, 11, 12, 13, 14, 15, 16, 17, 18, 19, 20, 21 (left),
    22 (world and background), 24, 25, 26 (bottom right), 27 (except top
    left), 28 (bottom), 29 (except top left and bottom right children)
Other images by Adobe Image Library

Library and Archives Canada Cataloguing in Publication

Kalman, Bobbie, 1947-
    We are the earth / Bobbie Kalman.

(Our multicultural world)
Includes index.
ISBN 978-0-7787-4634-8 (bound).--ISBN 978-0-7787-4649-2 (pbk.)

    1. Earth--Juvenile literature. I. Title. II. Series: Our multicultural world

QB631.4.K34 2009   j508   C2009-900485-2

Library of Congress Cataloging-in-Publication Data

Kalman, Bobbie.
    We are the earth / Bobbie Kalman.
        p. cm. -- (Our multicultural world)
    Includes index.
    ISBN 978-0-7787-4649-2 (pbk. : alk. paper) -- ISBN 978-0-7787-4634-8
(reinforced library binding : alk. paper)
    1. Earth--Juvenile literature. I. Title. II. Series.

QB631.4.K35 2009
508--dc22

                                                    2009002052

Crabtree Publishing Company

www.crabtreebooks.com   1-800-387-7650

Published in Canada
Crabtree Publishing
616 Welland Ave.
St. Catharines, Ontario
L2M 5V6

Published in the United States
Crabtree Publishing
PMB16A
350 Fifth Ave., Suite 3308
New York, NY 10118

Published in the United Kingdom
Crabtree Publishing
White Cross Mills
High Town, Lancaster
LA1 4XS

Published in Australia
Crabtree Publishing
386 Mt. Alexander Rd.
Ascot Vale (Melbourne)
VIC 3032

Contents

Earth is our home

Earth is the only **planet** in our **solar system** that has life. Only Earth has plants, animals, people, and other **living things**. Only Earth has air, water, and food. Earth is just the right distance from the sun, too. The sun gives all living things on Earth enough light and warmth to stay alive.

*The solar system is made up of the sun, planets, moons, and other things that float in space. The sun is at the center of our solar system. It does not move. The planets **orbit**, or move in circles, around the sun. Earth is the third-closest planet to the sun.*

We are the Earth!

Imagine looking at Earth from space! You would see no countries or **borders**. Earth is one planet. Every person, animal, and plant shares Earth. We are a part of everything, and everything is a part of us. We are the Earth!

Energy from the sun

The sun is a **star**. A star is a huge, hot ball of gas that glows. It warms Earth. **Energy** also comes from the sun. Energy is the power that living things need to move, grow, and stay alive. Living things are connected to other living things through sunlight! Plants use sunlight to make food (see page 12). When animals and people eat plants, the sun's energy is passed along. It is in everything we eat!

This girl is using the sun's energy to jump high in the air.

The sun's energy is in these grapes. It is in all the food we eat.

The sun keeps us warm. Its light contains the colors of the rainbow.

Light and color

The sun shines light onto Earth. Earth would always be very dark without the sun! Sunlight contains the colors we see in rainbows. The colors are red, orange, yellow, green, blue, indigo, and violet. All the colors we see in our world are made up of these colors.

On a sunny day, stretch your arms up to the sky and feel the sun's heat warm you. Can you feel the sun's energy flowing through your body?

Air is life

atmosphere

Earth is surrounded by layers of air that make up the **atmosphere**. The atmosphere is like a blanket of air around Earth. It protects us from the hot rays of the sun during the day. It also traps the sun's heat to keep Earth warm at night. The atmosphere contains the air we breathe. Without air, we could not survive for more than a few minutes.

*The atmosphere has the perfect mix of gases. Two of these gases are **oxygen** and **carbon dioxide**. Animals and people need to breathe oxygen. They **exhale**, or breathe out, carbon dioxide. Plants use the carbon dioxide in air to make food. They then give off oxygen. We need plants, and plants need us.*

Air connects us all

Breathing air connects us to other living things. We take about ten breaths every minute. Each breath we take has been breathed by other living things before! The oxygen in your last breath may have come from a tree in your back yard. Before that, the tree had used the carbon dioxide from another person or animal. The tree then gave off the oxygen you just inhaled.

All living things share Earth's air.

Thank you, air, for each breath I take!

The oxygen this boy is breathing may have come from the trees behind him. The carbon dioxide he exhales may be used to make food for the grass around him. A deer may eat the grass and also breathe the oxygen made by the grass. The children in the picture above might later breathe that same air.

Water bodies

Did you know that almost three-quarters (75 percent) of Earth is covered by water? Your body is made up of about 70-75 percent water, too. We are watery creatures living on a watery planet! Most of Earth's water is contained in oceans. Ocean water is **salt water**, but the water in rivers and lakes is **fresh water**. Fresh water does not contain a lot of salt. We need to drink fresh water to stay alive.

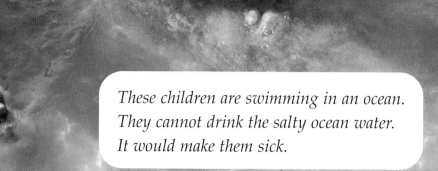

These children are swimming in an ocean. They cannot drink the salty ocean water. It would make them sick.

Moving and changing

The water we drink is **liquid** water. Liquid water flows. When water gets cold, it changes to **solid** ice or snow. When water gets hot, it **evaporates** and changes to **vapor**, or gas. It becomes part of the air. When we exhale, we give off water vapor as well as air. On very cold days, we can see the water vapor in our breaths.

water vapor

Connected by water

We are connected to other living things by water. The water vapor we exhale becomes part of clouds. The water in clouds may fall as rain or snow into oceans, rivers, or onto plants. Plants, animals, or other people then drink that water.

*This frog is on a leaf covered by drops of water called **dew**. Dew forms when water vapor cools and becomes liquid again. The frog will drink the dew. The dew may be part of the water vapor you exhaled in your breath last week.*

Gifts from plants

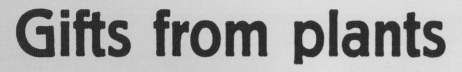

Plants use the energy of the sun to make food. Using sunlight to make food is called **photosynthesis**. Unlike plants, animals and people cannot make their own food. We get the sun's energy by eating plants or by eating animals that have eaten plants. Without plants, there would be no food! Plants give us delicious vegetables and fruits to eat. They shade us from the sun and freshen our air by making oxygen. Trees also provide homes for many kinds of animals. They provide the wood we use to build our homes, too.

sun

Plants use sunlight to turn carbon dioxide and water into food.

Plants give off oxygen for people and animals to breathe.

Plants give people food to eat. Many kinds of animals also eat plants.

A colorful world!

Flowers make the world a beautiful place to live. They come in many sizes, shapes, and colors. Flowers also smell wonderful! What is your favorite flower?

When you touch a flower, you touch the sun. When you smell a flower, you breathe clean, sweet air. When you look at a flower, you see the beauty in all living things—especially in yourself!

Amazing animals!

Animals can be as tiny as insects or as large as elephants. Animals live all over the world in many kinds of **habitats**, or natural homes. Some habitats are on land, and some are in water. Elephants live on land. Some birds, frogs, insects, and other animals live in trees. Fish, sea turtles, and whales live in oceans. Pets are animals that live in our homes.

butterfly (insect)

fish

snake

Humpback whales are huge animals that live in oceans.

pet kitten

tree frog

lovebirds

Endangered animals

Many animals are **endangered**. Endangered animals might soon disappear from Earth. Each time an animal is gone from Earth, nature is damaged because plants, animals, and people are all connected. We need one another, so losing animals also hurts us.

Elephants, leopards, sea turtles, and tuataras are endangered animals.

sea turtle

tuatara

leopard

The people connection

There are almost seven billion people on Earth. That is a lot of people! Earth's people are not all the same. They come from many different **cultures**. Culture is the way we live. It is the kinds of foods we eat, the way we dress, the beliefs we have, and the ways we celebrate. Culture is also the ways we show our imaginations through music, art, sports, and stories.

Dance is a part of culture. This girl is doing a Spanish dance called Paso Doble.

*This Korean family is wearing **traditional** clothing for a celebration. Traditional clothing is clothing that has been worn for hundreds of years. It is usually worn on special occasions.*

This boy is playing basketball. Sports are part of cultures, too.

16

We are all connected

People are different in some ways, but they are also the same. We have the same bodies and need the same things. We are connected to one another because we all live on Earth. Sometimes we forget that we are more alike than we are different. How can we feel more connected? We can get to know one another!

Getting to know you!

Getting to know people from different cultures is a great way to learn about the world and to connect with one another. We need to set aside our differences and work together to help care for Earth, our home. We need to feel more connected to **nature**, too. Where is nature? It is outdoors!

17

Nature is outdoors!

Do you learn about nature from books or television shows? Nature books and shows are a great way to learn about nature, but being outside in nature is the best way to feel connected to Earth. Get outdoors and see, hear, smell, touch, and taste nature!

This boy is standing in an ocean. He is watching some fish in the water. He feels them tickle his legs as they swim by.

Food seems to taste so much better when you eat it outdoors! Eating healthy foods makes you feel even more connected to nature. Why do you think that is?

Go for a hike in the woods. What sounds do you hear? Smell the fresh air that the trees around you are making. Balance on a fallen tree in the forest. Look for insects and mushrooms living on the log.

Learning from nature

No matter where we live, we depend on nature. No machine can make oxygen as well as a tree can, and trees make it for free. Nor can people make food using sunlight. We can learn how to make a cleaner, safer world by watching and copying nature.

These ants are working together to carry a heavy worm. Name five ways that we can work together to help Earth.

*The leaves of plants contain **chlorophyll**. Chlorophyll is a natural green color that catches the sun's energy so plants can make food. How can people catch more of the sun's energy?*

hyphae

*Mushrooms are not plants. They are living things called **fungi.***

*Some mushroooms are joined together under the ground by thin roots called **hyphae**. Hyphae connect with the roots of plants and help plants get more water and **nutrients** from the soil. They also clean the soil by breaking down dead wood and other plant parts. Why is healthy soil important to Earth?*

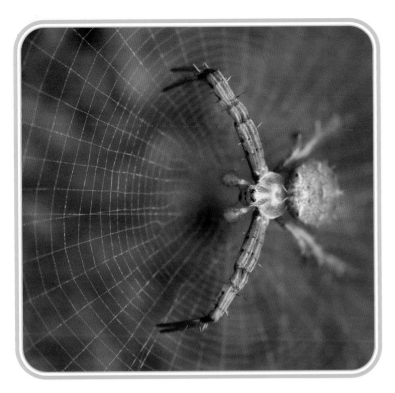

Spider webs are five times as strong as steel. Making steel **pollutes** the air and water, but spiders do not pollute when they make their webs. How can we copy spiders to create strong materials without pollution?

Nature-friendly

What can we learn from nature about living in ways that do not hurt Earth? Read this list and think of similar ways that you could be more nature-friendly!

- nature runs on sunlight
- nature does not waste energy
- nature does not waste anything
- nature **recycles** everything
- nature is always **adapting**, or changing, to the changes around it
- nature has many different parts, which are all important to one another

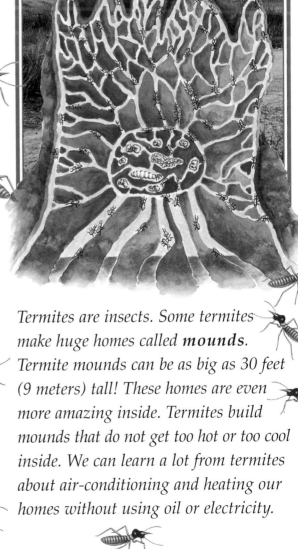

Termites are insects. Some termites make huge homes called **mounds**. Termite mounds can be as big as 30 feet (9 meters) tall! These homes are even more amazing inside. Termites build mounds that do not get too hot or too cool inside. We can learn a lot from termites about air-conditioning and heating our homes without using oil or electricity.

21

Earth's gifts to you

When you wake up in the morning, you stretch and yawn and take a deep breath. Do you think of air as a gift? You take a bath or shower and brush your teeth. Do you think of water as a gift? You get dressed and eat your breakfast. Do you think of food as a gift? Air is a gift. Water and food are gifts. Earth gives us all these gifts.

Attitude of gratitude

Gratitude is being thankful. It is a very powerful attitude. Gratitude is a way of knowing and feeling that everything in life is a gift. Each time we say "Thank you," we are showing respect for our gifts. Gratitude stops us from wasting the things for which we are thankful.

Gratitude power!

When you live with an attitude of gratitude, you become aware of what you really value in your life. You will be more **content**. To be content is to be peaceful and happy. Your happiness will make others happy, too. Happiness spreads quickly. Try it! You'll see that it's true!

We can show our gratitude to Earth by planting trees. Trees are gifts of fresh air, food, and homes for many animals. How else can we show our gratitude to Earth?

The Gratitude Dance

These animals look like they are dancing. Perhaps they are doing the Gratitude Dance! Make up your own Gratitude Dance and do it every day to thank Earth and to remind yourself of how wonderful your life really is!

praying mantis prance

grateful butterfly flutter

joyful froggy jump

bee thankful breakdance

owl appreciation twist

thankful kitten cha-cha

elephant gratitude waltz

What will you thank when you do your dance?

Thank you butterflies!

Thank you sun for my energy!

Thank you water!

Thank you legs!

Thank you air!

Thank you music!

Thank you laughter!

Thank you body!

Putting gratitude to work

You and your classmates have the power to change the world one person at a time. You are very powerful beings. You can do anything!

Gratitude makes us realize how fortunate we are to have food, clothes, homes, and schools. Part of gratitude is sharing our gifts with others who need our help. Many people on Earth do not have enough food to eat, clothes to wear, clean water to drink, or schools to attend. You and your classmates can work together as a team to find ways to help others. It is a way of putting your gratitude to work.

Helping others

Children are doing wonderful things to help people, animals, and the environment in their town and all over the world. They are helping dig wells, build schools, plant trees, and save endangered animals. Can you do great things, too?

Could you help build a school?

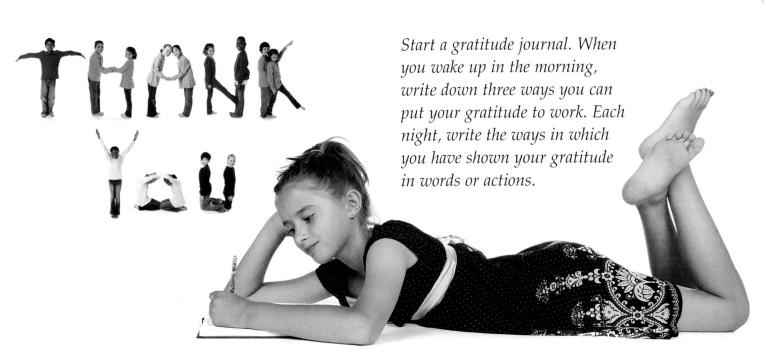

Start a gratitude journal. When you wake up in the morning, write down three ways you can put your gratitude to work. Each night, write the ways in which you have shown your gratitude in words or actions.

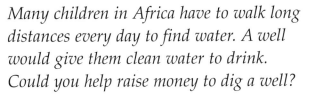

Many children in Africa have to walk long distances every day to find water. A well would give them clean water to drink. Could you help raise money to dig a well?

Could you volunteer to play with animals at an animal shelter?

Could you help save an endangered animal?

How can we be more ECO FRIENDLY?

Feeling grateful is a great step towards being **eco-friendly**. When we are eco-friendly, we do not hurt Earth or ourselves. Even making a few changes in our lives can make a big difference! As more people make changes, the world will become a cleaner, safer, more peaceful place for all living things.

Ask your parents to help you grow a vegetable garden in your yard. You will eat healthier food that will not have to travel in trucks and add pollution to our air.

Long ago, children planted vegetable gardens at school. Perhaps you and your classmates can learn more about the other eco-friendly things people did in pioneer times.

To recycle is to change used materials such as paper and plastic into new materials that can be used again. What do you recycle?

wind power

With your teacher and classmates, write letters to the government. Ask for more eco-friendly energy in your community!

Use a bike, scooter, or skateboard to go places, instead of asking your parents to drive you.

Use cloth bags instead of paper or plastic bags for carrying food and other things.

Buy used clothing and create your own style! You will save a lot of money, too!

Plant trees in your community.

Start a Green Club with your friends and challenge one another to do something eco-friendly every day!

Start with your heart!

Caring for Earth starts with our hearts. When we love Earth and one another, we can make our world a better place to live! We need to put our heads and hearts together to help save our beautiful planet. With your friends, make a plan to show your love for Earth. The positive statements on this page will help you get started.

Earth is our home. We love Earth!

We can work together!

We are grateful to Earth!

We are friends!

We are all GOOD!

We are the Earth!

We respect all living things!

We can do it. Yes, we can!

We are all important!

Glossary

Note: Some boldfaced words are defined where they appear in the book.

adapt To change in order to become better suited to a new environment or habitat

border A line that separates two countries

chlorophyll A green pigment found in plants that allows them to make food

evaporate To change a liquid, such as water, into vapor, or gas

fungi A group of living things, such as yeasts, molds, and mushrooms

habitat The natural place where a plant or animal lives

living thing Something that is alive

nature Outdoor areas that are not made by people, including plants and animals

nutrients Substances that help living things grow and stay healthy

photosynthesis The process by which plants use sunlight to make food from carbon dioxide and water

pioneer A person who is among the first to explore or settle in an area

planet A large object that rotates around the sun

pollute To add harmful waste, making an area unfit for living things

recycle To change old materials into new materials that can be used again

Index

Further reading

These books will help you learn more about how we can help Earth. For more information about the books, look for them in your library or go to **www.crabtreebooks.com**.

The ABCs of the Natural World series by **Bobbie Kalman**: Learn about endangered animals and about how you can help the environment in these books: *The ABCs of Endangered Animals*; *The ABCs of the Environment*. Reading level: grades 2–3.

Celebrations in My World series: *Earth Day* is about celebrating Earth, our home. We all share this beautiful planet! How can we show Earth our thanks?

 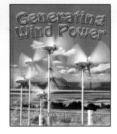 

Energy Revolution is a series that will give you information about alternative sources of energy. Books include: *Building a Green Community*; *Geothermal Energy: Using Earth's Furnace*; *How to Reduce your Carbon Footprint*; *Ocean, Tidal, and Wave Energy: Power from the Sea*; *Biomass: Fueling Change*; *Generating Wind Power*; *Harnessing Power from the Sun*; *Hydrogen: Running on Water*. Reading level: grades 4–5.

Environment Action! series encourages you to take an active part in caring for the environment in important ways: *Protect Nature*; *Recycle*; *Save Energy*; *Save Water*. Reading level: grade 4.

Green Team teaches you how to preserve the environment by challenging you to think before you hurt Earth with your actions. These fascinating books will motivate you to think and act "green!" *Reduce and Reuse*; *Using Energy*; *Using Water*; *Waste and Recycling*; *Your Food*; *Your Local Environment*. Reading level: grades 3–4.

 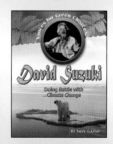 

Voices for Green Choices are stories about people who are working hard to create a cleaner Earth and inspiring us to do our part. *Al Gore: A Wake-Up Call to Global Warming*; *Rachel Carson: Fighting Pesticides and Other Chemical Pollutants*; *Victor Wouk: The Father of the Hybrid Car*; *David Suzuki: Doing Battle with Climate Change*; *Ed Begley, Jr.: Living Green*; *John Muir: Protecting and Preserving the Environment*. Reading level: grades 5–6.

Printed in the U.S.A.—CG